Pascal

A Journey with Autism

By Dr. Barbe Biloa - Many

Pascal: A Journey with Autism
Published by Yawn's Publishing
2555 Marietta Hwy, Ste 103
Canton, GA 30114
www. yawnspublishing.com

Library of Congress Control Number: 2019912363

ISBN: 978-1-947773-54-7 paperback
978-1-947773-55-4 eBook

Printed in the United States

Part I

Part II

Introduction

Dr. Biloa–Many (the author) takes the reader on the journey of Pascal, a young man with autism and his family who are dealing with an autism diagnosis, life, and treatment. We learn from their experience what it is like to live with autism. Pascal also promotes autism awareness. This book educates while updating us on the disability. Throughout the book, we learn how a family and the person with autism need support and comfort. We also realize how important autism awareness is today. Making people aware of autism should be a lifetime concern. It is shocking to find out that, even today, some families hear the word autism for the first time when their loved one is diagnosed. Keeping people aware of autism and other possible disabilities, therefore, is a concern for Dr. Biloa–Many. With the story of Pascal, the author, teaches us that autism is no longer a dead-end diagnosis; it is a starting point of a journey into a different way of living. With this book, the author hopes to help while educating people with and or without autism through Pascal and his family's autism journey and experience. The book might enable everyone interested in autism to acquire a basic understanding and knowledge not only about the disorder itself but also the challenges and strengths in the lives of people with autism. The book's goal is to finally enable families to deal with and cope with a child with autism. Obviously, a lot has already been said about autism, the lifetime condition. However, enough can never be said because year after year, children are being diagnosed with autism it is therefore important to keep people updated about researchers and other autism specialists or experts work to improve the life of people with autism. That is the reason why Dr.

Biloa-Many thinks that a new book on autism will always be welcome in keeping people aware and guiding them on what to do. With the high development of technology today, one would think people could easily google and surf the internet to find information and knowledge about autism, but not necessarily, as some people would rather read a book to learn from other real experience than surfing the internet. More and more autism awareness will help people understand that the disability need not be a complete mystery any longer.

The Purpose of this Book

Pascal is an inspiring real-life story of a young man with autism. Pascal's family and himself allowed the author to use his autism story for a specific purpose, which is to raise awareness and understanding of the Autism Spectrum Syndrome. Today around the world, everyone knows or is related to somebody with autism. Either a relative or a friend. Therefore, the audience of this book is composed of autism stake-holders, autism specialists, families with autistic children, etc. What really inspired the author to write this book is the growing rate of children diagnosed with autism around the world today. About one in fifty-nine children now have been identified with autism spectrum disorder (ASD) according to the CDC's Autism, and Developmental Disabilities Monitoring

(ADDM) Network CDC increases the estimate of autism's prevalence by fifteen percent, to one in fifty-nine children. (CDC 2017)

Everyone whether you have someone with autism today or not should learn a little bit about the disability. The reason being that if you don't have anyone with autism today that does not mean that you will not tomorrow. Another important fact about autism, everyone should be aware of is that according to the Autism Speaks Program, Autism is four to five times more common among boys than girls around the world. There are five autistic boys for each autistic girl. In other words, boys are five times more likely to be autistic than girls. CDC rates yield a gender ratio of about five boys for every girl The Centers for Disease Control and Prevention (CDC 2017) Studies show that if the first son is born with autism, there might be fifteen to twenty percent chance that the second child will have autism as well.

In this book, two persons will share what they know about autism and how they dealt with some autism situations. Pascal, the main character, will share his personal experience, and his mother will share her experience from a parent of a child with autism to advice and help other parents with autism. Finally, the author of the Book, Dr. Biloa–Many will jump in from time to time to share what she knows about the disability, from a general perspective related to its causes, prevention, treatments, increasing awareness and advocating for the needs of people with autism and their families.

Part I

What is Autism

Overview, Background, and Causes

Autism or autism spectrum disorder is also known as ASD. ASD will be used as the abbreviation to designate autism spectrum disorder throughout this book. ASD refers to a neurodevelopmental disorder or a range of conditions characterized by challenges with social skills, repetitive behaviors, speech, and nonverbal communication, as well as by unique strengths and differences. We have learned from researchers that there is not one autism type. As a result, we often hear the term spectrum used. The term spectrum means that not only are there different types of autism, but each child with autism is unique, and therefore, might be differently affected by the disorder and how he or she will present their unique characteristics. Autism, just like any other disability, has different causes. According to the American Autism Association (2016), scientists are not yet certain about what causes autism, but it's likely that both genetics and environment play a role. Autism according to the research (Autism Speaks Program 2016) appears to be caused by a combination of autism risk genes and environmental factors with a huge influence in the early brain development reflecting on the complexity of the disorder. There is a controversial debate about whether children are born autistic or not. Research states that autism as a neurological disability or developmental disorder which refers to brain development while the child is still in his or her mother's womb (Autism Speak Program 2016). In other words, autism has its roots in the very early brain development stage, meaning that kids are born autistic; they don't develop autism. The most obvious signs and symptoms appear between the age of two and three (Autism Speak Program 2016). Autism becomes apparent in toddlers or small children coincidence or fact; some of the toddlers diagnosed with autism presented their signs right after they get their vaccinations. Parents and families of children with autism have been confused with the controversy surrounding a link between vaccines and autism. In other words, in some cases, people believed that vaccines were the cause of their child's autism. There is no evidence from research today that Vaccines cause autism. Therefore, since there is no link between the MMR Measles, Mumps, and Rubella Vaccines and autism; parents should let their children get the immunization. The CDC Researchers (2014) and othcr autism specialists confirm that there is no evidence that the vaccine causes autism. In the author's opinion giving a child with autism the vaccine might trigger the not yet present evidence of autism. Even if it is believed that the real causes of autism are still unknown, it's accepted by most researchers that vaccines don't cause autism. However, researchers and clinicians argue that the debate over whether or not vaccines are a factor in the development of autism is far from settled because many families with children with autism insist and are confident that their child's development was normal until he or she received the shots.

Pascal, of course, was not an exception to that rule. Back then, research had not yet proven that vaccines do not cause autism. Pascal's mother believed that there was a link between Pascal's childhood vaccinations and his autism. His Mother recalls, he was a normal child until he received his first immunization. Right after, even though his speech was not fluent, he completely shut down. He lost his vocal ability and only gained it back after he was diagnosed with autism and put in multiple speech therapies. In other cases, the child sometimes remains nonverbal. Pascal's mother's first decision at that point, just like every parent of a child with autism thought back then, was to homeschool all her children at least in the preschool and elementary levels. She also decided to stop giving all of them any kind of shot, including the flu shot. Fortunately, a couple of years later when she was convinced that vaccines did not cause autism, she changed her mind about the vaccine and the homeschooling.

Just as children with autism do not present the same characteristics, the severity of their autism also varies in intensity from severe, mild to moderate and high functioning depending on which spectrum the child is affected by. Parents of children with autism should be confident that autism is not a disease but a disorder. In families with children with autism, research has not yet explained nor determined why one child might have autism and not the other children.

According to specialists, basic social interaction can be difficult for children with autism. They seem to live in their own world and can be completely detached from others. Children with autism are different from birth. The American Autism Association has identified the following symptoms for children with autism. Generally, children with autism: Will appear disinterested or unaware of others, they don't know how to connect with their peers or adults around them, they prefer not to be touched, have trouble understanding or talking about feelings and ignore when someone talks to them. They cannot make eye contact. Some children with autism spectrum disorders also have difficulty and delay with speech and language. They start talking late. However, parents should keep in mind that the ultimate goal for researchers and autism specialists is to help children with autism overcome their impairment or delay in social development, speech and language difficulties, tantrums or aggressive behavior if any.

Pascal's Symptoms of Autism

The Red flags

Pascal is a twenty-five-year-old young man with high functioning autism. He was born in Georgia in 1994, in a family of three children, two boys, and a girl. Pascal is the middle child and the only one with autism. Pascal's family lives in the countryside where his grandparents from his dad's side of the family own a farm. They have a fifteen-acre horse farm with seven stalls, five sheds, and twelve horses. The farm has five racehorses and five pleasure horses for fox hunting and driving. Pascal's family lived with his dad's extended family. Pascal's dad had four siblings, three brothers, and two sisters. Pascal's dad and his brother are lawyers, and they both took over their dad's law firm. Pascal's mom and his uncle's wife are paralegals, and both also work in the law firm. Pascal's other uncle is a medical doctor, and his wife is a nurse. His two aunties don't live on the farm; however, they live very nearby with their families. They had a total of eleven children, siblings and cousins together on the farm when Pascal was growing up. Sometimes eighteen when both aunties' children were over. Big family!!! There were a lot of children, siblings, and cousins around Pascal. Back in those days, autism in some parts of the country was either unknown or at its early stages of awareness. It all started for Pascal when at eighteen months old, his grandmother, who was also his babysitter, began to notice that there was something different about him. She would call him and would not get a response either with eye contact, smile, or even finger-pointing. Pascal could already, from time to time, say a word and sometimes could repeat a word that his grandmother used most often such as, eat, diaper and juice. Pascal also engaged in hand flapping and meltdowns about once every other day. Pascal's grandmother observed these symptoms. As time passed, she realized that he was not reaching his appropriate developmental milestones. He was developing differently than his siblings and cousins of the same age. Pascal's grandmother became very worried. She spoke with Pascal's parents first about his struggles and challenges. She was concerned that he might have autism. Obviously, a normal reaction from any parent would be denial. Pascal's parents were in denial. They did not believe the grandmother because, on the mom's side of the family, children were developing the same as Pascal. It was common, according to his mom to see her nieces and nephews not talk until after they were three years old. Pascal's Mother heard the word autism for the first time from her mother-in-law and decided to more closely observe him and do some research. Once she learned a little bit about autism, she then noticed the lack of recognition in Pascal's eyes. She noticed that he also had a hard time eating and sleeping. As each day passed, she recognized more and more red flags that characterized autism in some of Pascal's repetitive behaviors and delays in speech and sound. As Pascal grew older, and after he received his MMR vaccines, he struggled even more with some of the challenges associated with having ASD; including a speech impediment and communication difficulties. Then and only then, was his family convinced that something in Pascal's milestone development was not right, and they needed to find out why. Pascal's parents finally decided to take him to see several doctors and an autism specialist. Even if they suspected autism,

Pascal's family held out hope that his diagnosis process would prove otherwise. Which, unfortunately, was not the case. Pascal was referred for the autism diagnostic process. Pascal said, "my mother finally agreed to ask my pediatrician and my uncle, who is a doctor, for an evaluation." Some of Pascal's red flags was the fact that he could not have big smiles or other warm, joyful expressions, no back-and-forth sharing of sounds, smiles, or other facial expressions. "I did not babble, did not have any gestures like pointing, showing, mocking, reaching, or waving goodbye either. Finally, I had not spoken hardly a word, not even any meaningful two or three-word phrases, including imitating or repeating by twenty-four months." As already stated above, the range and severity of autism characteristics vary widely. Each child with autism looks different. However, common symptoms of autism are delays or difficulty with social skills, along with communication and excessive repetitive behaviors according to the (Autism Speaks Program (2016)).

Generally, parents, family members, close friends, relatives, pediatricians, or teachers are often the first ones to notice that a child is showing either unusual behaviors or delays in his or her development. So, if someone close to a child shows concern, that person should recommend that the parents ask the child's doctor for a referral to either a developmental pediatrician or an autism specialist. Information about who and when to call is now available to the public through the Autism Speaks website and resources guide (Autism Speaks, 2016).

Pascal's Diagnostic Process

Whenever a pediatrician notices a delay in a child's milestone, he/she should make the recommendation to have the child evaluated. Pascal's mother learned that every child's diagnosis is different. However, a child autism diagnosis is based on either his or her lack of a milestone or an uncommon behavior or skill. According to Pascal's mom, things started off as normal as they could be for their family. Suddenly, he shut down and was still not speaking much by the age of three, and he was showing excessive aggressive behavior and tantrums instead. Autism specialists consider these as a delay in an age-appropriate milestone along with repetitive behaviors. The Individual with Disabilities Education Act (IDEA 1998) states that every child with autism and or other disability is entitled to a free evaluation from either a state agency or the Department of Education before the child is twenty years old. However, some parents prefer to take their children to a private specialist, a developmental pediatric doctor, a psychiatrist, or any known medical professional or autism specialist for a second or third opinion. Pascal's mother first talked to his pediatrician, and he recommended that she schedule an appointment with a doctor who specifically deals with developmental issues in children.

ASD can sometimes be detected as early as eighteen months or later, but by age two, a diagnosis by an experienced professional should be considered very reliable. However, in some cases, children do not receive a final diagnosis until they are three years old. (American Autism Association (2016))

Diagnosing autism can be difficult and generally

consists of two steps: developmental Screening and the comprehensive Diagnostic Evaluation American Psychiatric Association (2013). Pascal's diagnosis process took a couple of months and consisted of the following steps and process: Developmental Screening and Comprehensive Diagnostic Evaluation

The Developmental Screening

In Pascal's case, his mother stated that his Developmental screening was a short test to find out if he has reached his basic skills milestone, or he has delays and difficulty reaching that milestone. Pascal said, "during the developmental screening, the doctor asked my parents some questions. They talked and played with me during an examination to see how I learn, speak, behave, and move." A delay in any of these areas could be a sign of a problem. It is important for doctors to screen all children for developmental delays, but especially to monitor those who are at a higher risk for developmental problems. Today things are set up in the way that, every child, autistic or not can be screened early for developmental delays and or other disabilities during each of his or her regular well-child doctor visits. "Parents today also consent to have their children specially screened for ASD during their regular well-child doctor visits," Pascal's mom added. "If a child is at risk for ASD because his or her sibling already have autism or the child himself present behaviors associated with autism, specifics additional screening should be recommended during the doctor's well-child visit or A referral to a comprehensive diagnostic evaluation."

The Comprehensive Diagnostic Evaluation

A comprehensive evaluation is the second step of diagnosis (American Psychiatric Association 2013). "The comprehensive diagnostic evaluation for Pascal," his mother explained "consisted of a thorough evaluation and review of his behavior and his milestones development. It also consisted of a parental interview. Pascal was also given hearing, vision, and other neurological testing and screening."

"A parental interview is when my doctor asks my parents questions about my medical background, the symptoms that she has noticed and what made her suspect it was autism. And, of course, she also asked about both sides of the families' medical and mental history. Finally, they needed to mention the symptoms my grandmother noticed, and when she began to notice them, and more importantly, the frequency and the severity of these symptoms. After the parental interview came the medical examination. It all started as a routine doctor visit, and then the doctor added a neurological examination, along with genetic testing. The doctor also recommended that I take a hearing test and lead screening. According to him, trouble hearing can also affect children's language and social skills. Hearing issues can sometimes lead to a hearing impairment with similar symptoms as autism. The doctor then told my mom that I needed to be observed by everybody and during that observational period data should be recorded wherever I was in order to detect any abnormal behavior and its triggers in different settings and environments. The doctor wanted to know how I was interacting with the people around me. The observational period with the doctor consisted of him handing me a specific toy or snack, then watching to see how I would play with the toy or eat the snack.

"After these first series of tests, my doctor chose to run more tests; the cognitive assessment test, a speech evaluation with a speech therapist and a sensory–motor tasks test. My comprehensive psychological evaluation consisted of a formal assessment of intellectual abilities and an assessment of adaptive behavior. My educational evaluation test consisted of an assessment of my educational performance and my current functioning levels. My communication evaluation was an assessment of my verbal and nonverbal communications. My behavioral evaluation test consisted of an assessment of my social interaction and participation in my peer and adult interactions."

Parents could also request a self-referral to the first steps program if they suspect that their child may be autistic. The child who is suspected of having autism will then be evaluated by an eligibility team, usually a group of qualified health care professionals and the parents. The evaluation can take sixty to one hundred and thirty-five minutes (The Centers for Disease Control and Prevention (CDC 2017)), and it is conducted in an environment familiar and comfortable to the child, such as at home, or at his or her daycare. During the evaluation, the team uses the assessment Evaluation, and Programming System or the AEPS, and the team observes the child and his family interact while a parental interview is done. This happened in Pascal's case. The team gathered information and data to be used at a program eligibility meeting. If the child falls below a required criterion for a developmental area such as communication or his motor skills, the team will then conclude that the child is eligible for the first steps program. Pascal explains, "with my parents' consent to that first steps program; my team developed a plan for intervention, also called the Individualized Family Service Plan or IFSP. Later on, when I went to school, I was provided a speech therapist, and an occupational or physical therapist was also selected."

According to Pascal's mom, his diagnosis of autism remains behavioral. Doctors and other healthcare professionals rely only on observation and information from several sources such as parents, physicians, and therapists because she believes back then and even today there is not yet a medical test that specifically diagnoses autism. The manual used to evaluate and determine if Pascal met the requirements for an autism spectrum was the Diagnostic and Statistical Manual (DSM-5). Fortunately, or unfortunately, he did meet the evaluation criteria. However, at the end of testing if the child meets the criteria, parents should be strongly involved by talking to the doctors and health professionals on their child's team about the prognosis and decide with them the best way to proceed for treatment, Pascal's mom advised.

The results of Pascal's assessments and evaluation confirmed his autism diagnosis. In 1998, at four years old, Pascal was declared a child with high-functioning autism. Obviously, his parents and extended family members were very concerned and worried. Pascal's family journey into this world of autism began with his diagnosis.

Pascal's diagnosis came as a relief to his entire family because it explained his behavior. His family understood why he was acting different and why he could not easily make or keep friends. It's was a bittersweet feeling. Bitter because it's kind of sad but sweet in the way that it explained a lot of Pascal's unusual behavior.

Once Pascal was diagnosed with autism, the family, including his uncle, the doctor, had no clues, no knowledge nor education whatsoever about the disability or disorder. They were all confused and worried about the mysteries surrounding the word autism. The worst thing is that they had no idea where to begin or when and where it would end if it would ever end. Back in those days, people were not aware and did not have any knowledge or education about ASD. This was very common within families of children with autism. With the diagnosis, Pascal's family had to quickly move to the next step, which was thinking about how to handle and live with a child with autism. That included learning and knowing the services and support the family would need in order to be the best advocate for their child. No one is ever prepared for a child's diagnosis of autism, even when parents are concerned with their child's development difficulties or because the child is showing some or all of the signs or symptoms described above. Pascal's family was shocked, of course; who wouldn't be? They experienced a range of emotions that led to the answers to the following questions:

What is autism? Why them anyway? What will their son's life, as well as the family's life with him, now turn into? What had God decided to get them into? As a religious family, they had to view it from a religious perspective, and his parents could not have helped themselves thinking that they must be getting a punishment from God for not having been fully practicing their faith. They blamed each other; then they put the blame on the vaccines. They did not know if there was any kind of hope for Pascal's future. The thought of him having to miss any life experience, from enjoying birthday's parties to playing sports, dating his first girlfriend, prom, graduation, getting a driver's license, or getting married and having his own children was devastating and heartbreaking to the family. "My heart would not stop pounding! It was so painful, and I wanted my son to get better right away," Pascal's mother exclaimed. "At some point, I even questioned my faith, because I could not understand why my God would let something like that happen to my son," she added. the author believes that these are normal feelings associated with grieving from an autism diagnosis.

However, parents and other extended family members must learn to cope with the fact that their child has autism.

Feeling and Coping

The news that a child has autism is devastating to the family. It is not easy news to hear and process. It was not easy for Pascal's family in the late 90s; it is not now and will never be for a family of a child with autism. The diagnosis of a child's developmental disorder, such as autism, is always very emotional, confusing, troubling, and challenging for parents. Today, parents and families of children with autism all agree that not only did they all react differently to their child's autism diagnosis, but also to each other. As far as Pascal's parents were concerned, they admitted that their feelings included, either a big shock, a relief, and of course sadness and worries when their fear was confirmed. To each other, they felt angry, frustrated, self-blaming, and guilt that the other parent might be responsible for the child's diagnosis. The diagnosis enables parents and families to understand better their child differences and difficulties as well as what they need to do to help the child. Parents should, for instance, think about the next step, which is to be educated on the disability. It is often said that knowledge is power. Parents should understand that the more they know, the better they will be able to handle their child's disability. There are so many autism organizations and support groups available out there for parents that they should not feel isolated about helping their child. The autism diagnosis of a child, without doubt, can put the relationship between both his or her parents on the line. Many stressors can have an influence on the parent's marriage. It is obvious that each parent or relative is affected and will react and respond differently to their child's autism diagnosis. In Pascal's case, his mother said that she and her husband felt guilty, sad, and even angry. Obviously, those are normal reactions for parents who understand and know the lifelong impact of autism on their child and family because they are human beings with emotions. Other parents from Pascal's mother's support group told her that they blamed each other, and they finger pointed to each other's family history and background for the cause of that diagnosis. What couples need to realize here is that these feelings are appropriate reactions to expect from the news that your child has autism. However, they should try very hard to move on and focus on the process that will help the child and the family. This is, of course, easier said than done, Pascal's mother thought. "Parents should not let their negative feelings about autism last too long if they do it might pull them apart and in some cases even cause the marriage to end," Pascal's mom pointed out.

Some parents told Dr. Many that their child's diagnosis was the primary cause of their divorce. The author believes that, instead of keeping them apart, the child's autism diagnosis should make the parents very strong, and very close to each other. This will be possible if the rest of the family steps in to help and support the parents because they might not always express what they are going through even if they really need support and advice. Unfortunately, some parents think they should keep their child's diagnosis a secret from their family and friends because they fear their reactions and emotions. This might not be the right decision. The extended families' members support is very helpful and beneficial to parents. Each one of the family's members, especially if they want to help, has a lot to offer. At some point, the parents should stop grieving. Of course, they cannot permanently push it away; it will come back from time to time as long as they are dealing with autism along the way. “However, someone, no matter who, in the family it may be, the dad, the mom, grandad, grandma, uncles or aunties, needs to step up and let the couple know that it is time to move forward and think about what to do next, where and when to start now,” Pascal’s mom said. In their case, Pascal’s dad took the lead and acknowledged that the problem was serious, and they needed an appropriate and strong strategy to tackle and handle it. Pascal’s mom did more research about autism and its services and resources through conference, training, and books. Getting all this information was very overwhelming, but she had no other choice than doing it. She stated that she remembered having to cry whenever she was alone. She thought she was hiding her sadness from Pascal’s siblings and cousins. She could not have imagined how quickly they noticed that something was either wrong or was bothering her. She was no longer the joyful mom and aunt she used to be. All the children on the farm were very happy around her. They were all asking what was going on with her. They could not recognize her anymore. Then and only then did she become strong and said to herself that enough was enough. She needed to have the strength to deal with autism for the sake of her family. Pascal's parents' grief process lasted about a couple of months after he was diagnosed with autism. Managing their reaction and emotions was very challenging. They finally came up with a strategy that enabled them to focus on helping Pascal and the family. They both agreed that for a while, the mom needed to stop working to have enough time for Pascal and for the rest of the family. "Obviously, giving up my job was the greatest life change for me," Pascal's mom said.

Just like a regular teenager in America, she had her financial independence ever since she was eighteen years old. Now, she would depend only on her husbands income. Some other mothers said they had to reduce their working hours instead. There are no standard right or wrong strategies, as long as there are open communication and negotiation between parents for the sake of the child with autism and the family. In other words, according to the author, every family is their own judge. Parents should go with whatever plan they feel is best for the family because they are their child's main caregiver. They need a lot of time between medical and or therapy appointments on a daily basis, along with handling the need of the family. Parents also need to think about themselves as a couple. Pascal's mom reported that one mistake they made as parents was to put only Pascal's needs in the center of the family's life.

They understood later on that their family's life should not revolve around Pascal's needs only. Of course, that is very hard, especially in the beginning; parents and family are willing to do whatever it takes, even putting their own needs and the needs of the rest family on hold to take care of their child with autism. They quickly changed their minds once they realized that this is a lifetime condition. They wanted Pascal to get better so much, and they thought it would happen right away. Couples or parents of a child with autism should consider spending time together. Especially with the overwhelming demands of their child that they experience on a daily basis. Parents need to find that time alone where they can sit and relax, even if it is only an hour per weekend. As much as possible, couples should keep up with their regular activities together. In Pascal's case, his mother reported that once a week she and her husband went on a date either Friday, Saturday or Sunday evening. The next weekend they would do something different; go out for dinner, to the movies, travel to visit friends or other families with children with autism. The time that a couple spends together alone reinforces their bond and makes their relationship or marriage healthier and stronger. Another thing parents of children with autism should consider is asking for help as needed, as well as keeping a helpful support group. Parents should not be afraid to seek help from friends, extended family members, or caregivers. Pascal's mother stated that most of the support that they needed from their extended family members, grandparents, uncles, aunts, cousins were right there on the farm from her husband's side, her own family and friends who did not live on the farm were a great support as well.

Why? Because they shared every single step with their family from Pascal's different behavior to his autism diagnosis. Pascal's mom added that they had no other choice anyway, since not only they all lived on the farm, but also it was her mother-in-law, Pascal's grandmother, who first noticed that something was not right with Pascal's development. She was very suspicious about Pascal having autism. She knew more than anyone else in the family that every single step of a child's developmental milestones was different with Pascal. When they had the diagnosis, Pascal's mom could not stop repeating over and over that it was an explanation and a big relief for the entire family on both sides from all their years of doubt, questions and denial. Pascal's mom stated that in term of extended family support, their in-laws made themselves available for Pascal, which was a great relief for the parents. They barely had to ask for help because the help system that the family put in place allowed everyone to spend time alone with Pascal. They were very lucky and grateful for that. "We could not have done without that support," Pascal's mom added. However, for the parents and families of children with autism who are not as fortunate as Pascal's parents, they should seek help and support as stated above as needed from their family, relatives, friends, extended family members and caregivers. Help and support will give them some time alone together as a couple and away from their child with autism. It is very important and will keep the couple's relationship or marriage strong. All parents with or without a child with autism needs someone to rely on; someone who they know has their back. That is the reason why everyone has friends, and everyone goes back home to their parents and extended family members when they have them around. That need for someone to depend on or to rely on is even greater when the family dynamic changes because of a child with autism. Parents should always keep in mind and let the extended family members know that the responsibility of raising a child with autism is a team responsibility. Working together in raising a child with autism while they managed other household responsibilities has created a stronger bond between parents. Other parents stated that they went to counseling before they had a support group because their family members lived out of town. The counselor helped and supported them whenever necessary and even gave them a break when needed. Counselors are another option available for parents. Couples and partners should never be afraid nor hesitate to seek counseling. Research shows that they are professional, and they might better determine and identify the needs of a family with an autistic child. As already stated before, it is a relief for everyone who expresses their feelings to someone like a counselor who will listen and address them. "The memories of raising a child with autism last a lifetime. They will never leave your mind," Pascal's mom said. She said to this day, she still remembers like it was yesterday those periods of intense anxiety after they received the diagnosis; Pascal's first day of school in his special education class, his first therapy day, the day that they had to tell and explain to their others kids, nieces and nephews that Pascal has autism, and living with him will bring a huge change to the entire family and extended family life. According to Pascal's mom, there is no standard way to a successful marriage or relationship for parents and couples with autistic children. Her advice to parents and couple is to keep connected, work as a team and ask for help and advice as needed in order to decrease the stress and or depression associated with raising a child with autism. Today, things are much better with research and other autism experts' and specialists' work. Even if all the answers are not yet provided, parents and families of children with or without autism are well aware of the disability, and they can now easily tackle the bumps along the autism journey. The autism ride is usually a little bumpy; however, parents can overcome it. With research, parents and families have access to traditional and contemporary approaches that enable them to successfully raise and change the course of their kids with autism life. That is the reason most parents and other professionals keep their hopes up on treatments and different intervention methods that contribute to making a significant difference by improving the outcomes of children and adults with autism.

Pascal's Treatments Options

Once a child is diagnosed with autism, the next step is to identify and start the appropriate "treatment" and services for him or her. This step consists of providing an early intervention program for the child. Experts and other autism specialist agree that the earlier the intervention starts, the better the child's brain development will be. We often hear that early intervention in autism is the key. What is early intervention? Early intervention treatments are a range of appropriate and critical services that are provided by autism specialists to a child with autism to help him or her learn developmental skills and lead to a better outcome (Kasari, C., & Patterson, S. 2012). These services are assistive technology, speech and language therapy, occupational and physical therapy, psychological therapy. The services also address the family's needs and priorities for their child. It is important to know that early intervention programs are provided under the Individuals with Disabilities Act (IDEA) free or at low cost for children with disabilities and autism. Early intervention services will help any child with autism from birth to three years old (thirty-six months) learn or improve important skills. Services include therapy with a specialist that helps the child talk, walk, and interact with others. "Therefore, it is always very important to talk to the child's doctor as soon as possible if you suspect that your son or daughter has an ASD or other developmental problem," Pascal's mom said. It is important for parents to know that even if your child has not been diagnosed with an ASD yet, he or she may still be eligible for early intervention treatment services. The Individuals with Disabilities

Education Act for children (IDEA,2011) says that children under the age of three years (thirty-six months) who are at risk of having developmental delays may be eligible for services. These services are provided through an early intervention system in any state. Through this system, you can ask for an evaluation. Treatment for particular symptoms, such as speech therapy for language delays, often one does not need to wait for a formal ASD diagnosis. While early intervention is the key, intervention at any age as soon after diagnosis as possible is critical. Early intervention programs are different in structure, treatment goals, and curriculum and hours, depending on each child's needs and age. "By law, every child with autism has a specific Individual Family Service Program (IFSP) (IDEA,2011)," Pascal's mom said. The IFSP is a document that spells out the child's treatment plan with the Early Intervention services (EI) that the child should receive. The IFSP also defines the child's levels of functioning, her or his specific needs as well as his or her objectives and goals for treatment (IDEA,2011). "Pascal's IFSP described his current levels of functioning and the anticipated goals. It also listed the specific services that will be provided to him and our family," his mom stated. "In details, Pascal's IFSP program included: our involvement as parents, intensive playful social interaction with the speech therapist, and play activities to meet learning goals and objectives," Pascal mother added. Pascal had all types of treatment available out there. You name it; he had it. His mother would not skip any treatment available for him. His treatments were classified into two categories; the first one was behavior and communication approaches; the second one was medical approaches. With a child with autism, parents and families learn and embrace new terms such as treatment or therapies or intervention. Parents should be familiar with the autism vocabulary because the autism-specific terms are used interchangeably throughout the process to describe the child's specific treatment. Once again, just like each child with autism is unique, so is each child's intervention plan. The IFSP describes the child's current level and defines the appropriate services to support both his or her development and the family's responsibility to help the child's development and achieve a better outcome. Researchers have developed different effective early intervention models. However, the applied behavior analysis (ABA), is the most common effective behavioral and communication method. The ABA approaches that help children with ASD are those that provide structure, direction, and organization for the child in addition to family participation

Autism Speak (2016). ABA has become widely accepted among health care professionals and is used in many schools and treatment clinics. ABA encourages positive behaviors and discourages negative behaviors to improve a variety of skills. The child's progress is tracked and measured. In Pascal's case, his therapies consisted of a wide range of teaching methods that his dad and mother chose for him to reach his full potential. Services for Pascal included speech and language instruction, occupational therapy, physical therapy, Applied Behavior Analysis (ABA), and psychological evaluation. "Services for my family, on the other hand, included training for us to help reinforce his new skills and counseling to help the family adapt," his mother explained. In the EI program (Early Intervention), Pascal was under the care and support of caring professionals well known for their expertise in autism treatment. With therapies, he learned how to verbalize his thoughts and feelings through speech, and he also learned how to socialize with others through the use of basic games. "I later understood that the purpose of the games was to teach him how to play with others and keep his sensory needs in mind. I particularly like the tickling game for Pascal, because I could see that he was getting the stimuli that he needed to regulate himself," she added. According to his mother, Pascal also received structured therapeutic activities for thirty hours per week as required by law. Pascal's ABA sessions were two to three hours long every day, sometimes in the morning, sometimes in the afternoon. Each session consisted of short periods, five minutes of structured time for an activity, for example, letting him draw, or putting a puzzle together. He could not read at the time, but the therapist would let him look at a picture book if he wanted to. Then he would get a fifteen-minute break per hour with free play time as a reward if the activity was done successfully. Also, Pascal received related services. His mother described those services as therapies that address symptoms associated with autism. For Pascal, they consisted of Occupational Therapy (OT) for skills that he would need to live as independently as possible. Skills might also include dressing, eating, bathing, and relating to people. Sensory Integration Therapy for sensory information, like sights, sounds, and smells. Sensory integration therapy could help a child who is bothered by certain sounds or does not like to be touched. Speech Therapy to help improve his communication skills. Some people can learn verbal communication skills. Luckily for Pascal, he regained his voice after his therapies. For other nonverbal children, the use of gestures or picture boards would be more appropriate and realistic to improve their communication. Another communication device is The Picture Exchange Communication System (PECS). Pascal did not need the PECS. PECS uses picture symbols to teach communication skills, mostly to nonverbal children with autism. The child, during the therapy session, is taught how to use picture symbols when asking and answering questions or just having a conversation. It helps nonverbal children with autism to communicate their need. Technology today is so advanced that there are multiple communication software options available for televisions, tablets, game systems, and even phones to help children with autism communicate. Physical Therapy (PT) for Pascal, on the other hand, focused on addressing any problems with his movement that could cause any of his functional limitations. By law, PT can address poor muscle tone, balance, and coordination. According to his mom, Pascal's physical therapist first evaluated his developmental level and abilities in order to design appropriate activities that targeted his need and abilities. Pascal's PT then consisted of assisted movement, various forms of exercise, and orthopedic equipment usually delivered during a thirty minute to one-hour session every day. For some children with ASD, a strong medical intervention may also be required, but his mom said Pascal did not need any. He was prescribed only a psychopathic medication supposedly for his mood swings in school. Pascal also had an individualized education program (IEP). The IEP designed Pascal's educational needs, related services, goals, and objectives. Pascal's IEP team (teachers, school administrators, and related services personnel) worked with the family to improve Pascal's educational results. The IEP is the cornerstone of a quality education for each child with ASD. Parents and families of children with autism will do anything possible to improve their journey through autism, even changing the family's diet. That is the reason why they adopt a gluten-free diet as a home remedy for autism. "Obviously, I did not know anything about such a diet. I have never even heard about the gluten-free diet before. I had to google, read, and learn about the diet and its possible effect on children with disabilities," Pascal's mother admitted. "Then I talked to parents who already had their kids with autism on a gluten-free diet to find out their thoughts about the diet so that I could learn from their experiences. All of them agreed that the gluten-free diet had a great outcome for their child with autism. I also asked Pascal's pediatrician, as well as our EI team members, we reviewed and discussed the potential risk and or benefits and established measurable outcomes. However, I did not put Pascal on the gluten-free diet right away," his mother stated. When he was six years old, Pascal's mom explained how Pascal started having chronic diarrhea. He was throwing up, had headaches, stomach cramps with a lot of gas, and sleeping issues. His pediatrician put him on all kinds of medicine, but nothing worked. "I recalled the pediatrician's frustration over the medication that usually worked to treat his symptoms on other kids but did not work for Pascal. The pediatrician finally referred us to a gastrointestinal specialist, unfortunately, who tried to treat his symptoms for nearly a year with no positive results either. Pascal's allergy test did not reveal any food allergy or intolerance, and his symptoms barely improved, and they stayed recurrent. I learned from a parent in my support group that I should consult a dietician. She referred me to her dietician. Then, and only then, did we decide to put my family on a gluten-free diet," his mother said. "The dietician gave me a list of what my children could eat and where to find these gluten-free products. A couple of months on the gluten-free diet improved Pascal's symptoms, and as time went by, all the digestion symptoms were gone. Let me mention that the gluten-free diet does not help with autism, but, in Pascal's case, but in Pascal case, the gluten – free diet helped with the digestion problems associated with autism.," his mom clarified. "The big challenge back in those days was where to find gluten-free products. They were only available in some health food stores, and of course, they were very expensive.

The gluten-free diet improved my family's life so much that my brothers, sisters, and in-laws adopted the diet for their families. I can't imagine us going back on a regular diet. The gluten-free diet is working perfectly for us. Today, the diet is so much easier and affordable!" Pascal's mom exclaimed. "Whatever you need gluten-free can be found in any grocery store. Just look for the gluten and dairy free labels or aisle sections. Some restaurants also have gluten-free or dairy-free options on their menu today. My kids drank almond or coconut milk, but anything else was gluten-free: pasta, bread, crackers, cakes, cereal, and other stuff from the bakery. You need to know that gluten-free, like organic products, is expensive. You will need to spend a little more money than with your regular groceries and food."

Part II

Pascal's Journey

The second half of this book talks about Pascal at home, Pascal at school and Pascal as an adult today. Research shows that children with autism behave differently at school and at home, In Pascal's case, his mother believed that some days, and for some reasons, he found school very stressful but kept his emotions and feelings for home. She could not determine what triggered the behavior that occurred at home after school. As Pascal grew up, his parents, just like any other parents back in the day, worried about what his life will be as an adult. That is the focus of this part of the book.

Pascal at Home

Pascal explains, "Before I was diagnosed, no one except my grandmother could have imagined why I was acting out. To my parents, siblings, and extended family, it was kind of confusing and frustrating. After the diagnosis, everything made a lot more sense because they all knew and understood what I had been going through and how we all had to deal with it in the family. My family quickly realized that they needed to be able to help and take preventive measures. At first, it felt like living in a complete whole new world. Today, my parents, siblings, and extended family can proudly say that living in the autism world made us all better people. We learned patience. My siblings and some of my cousins took control. They introduced me to things and got me involved. They wouldn't let me use autism as a crutch or excuse for not being involved. I would get into fights with my siblings and cousins, but being able to make-up and process what happened was different for me compared to the rest of them. For me, when the fight was over, the board was erased clean. In other words, a couple of minutes later, everything was completely back to normal. Sometimes, it seemed to my family like I was doing it to annoy them, but that wasn't the case. I wasn't doing it on purpose. It was very hard for them to understand how I could easily get over a fight. Experiences like this made me learn to be more understanding and also learn that people handle things differently. My advice for siblings and cousins of people with autism would be to have empathy and patience. For my family and relatives, living with me was a huge practice of those values. As a young man with Autism Spectrum Disorder today, looking back when it all first started, I will tell you that I've come a long way. I can reflect today on both the challenges and strengths that my condition has led me to.

"My mother always said that I was a happy little boy when everything was fine and the most distressing and stressful kid anyone could imagine as soon as something went wrong or did not go my way. At that time, more than twenty years ago, not everyone knew about autism disorder, and few interventions were available. According to mom, I was a playful and affectionate baby. I was a little fat, and not everyone could pick me up. Everybody thought that since I was so heavy, I would have delays walking, or even crawling. Nope, they were wrong because at six months old, I started to sit up and crawl in my crib, then on the floor. I attended daycare twice a week, and at the daycare, by the time I was nearly a year old, I could walk and say some words even though they were not clear, but at least they sounded like words. Everything seemed "normal" until that fateful Saturday afternoon when I was found by my mother sitting alone in the garage, repeatedly spinning the wheels of my bike with such persistence and concentration, that when she called me, I did not respond. I did not even acknowledge her presence in the garage. I was eighteen months old. From that day on, I became a different infant. I stopped babbling; I was running around the house and the farm knocking everybody's stuff down in my way; breaking my siblings' toys. And I would throw a tantrum whenever I was asked or made to stop. When told no, I would kick, bite, and even try to fight my siblings and cousins. The reason for these behaviors is that I was autistic. I was born autistic.

"For my mother, a summary of a day with me looked like this: The day of my therapy, she would pick me up from school, and we would go for my therapy session. Then, we would get back home, and I would take my nap. After my nap, I would eat my snack, then have any of my leisure activities. Then we would eat dinner, and after dinner, I would fix my lunch for the next day of school and take my bath. I preferred bathing at night, right before bed. Some nights, if my mom was not watching me, I would not take either a shower or a bath. Somchow, the next morning, my mom would notice that I skipped my shower. Without me knowing, she started watching me, and one night I thought she was already asleep, and I went to the bathroom for a couple of minutes and came right back out. She was standing in my room, waiting for me. When I walked in, she checked my towel, and of course, it was completely dry since I did not use it. She knew right away why the towel was not wet. I did not shower. From that night on and up to today, I shower twice a day; mornings and evenings. That was the only way for my mom to be sure that I was going to get my daily shower. My grandmother once asked her why I needed two showers every day, and she replied that if I skipped one shower some days, I would at least have the other one which would be enough for a day.

"I'm on a gluten-free diet, so I had to take my lunch every day. I don't know if it is true, but it seems like people with autism don't like bathing or showering but love to eat. I have such a great appetite that my siblings and cousins thought I had an eating disorder. A first I thought that it was just me, then I realized that it is a common characteristic for children with autism. A lot of my friends talked about how they ate a lot and would not shower unless they were reminded to. Some other parents of children on the spectrum told the same thing to my mom, which is weird because I had no problem getting in the pool. I love swimming, but I just don't love a bath or shower. That said, let's get back to my daily routine. My mother would wake me up every single morning. If she did not, I would not get up. They tried everything, setting the alarm, having my sibling wake me up; nothing worked. I would only wake up when my mom woke me up. Don't ask me why. I don't know. When I think about that today, I believe she had her special technique to easily get me out of bed. However, over the weekend, I would independently wake up. I did not need any assistance to get out of my bed on Saturday and Sunday mornings. Once I was up, I would do my hygiene, then take my morning shower or bath. By the time I got downstairs, my mother had already fixed breakfast for the family. On weekdays, I would have breakfast, take my meds, and get on the bus. After school, if I did not have anything going on like doctor's appointments or therapy, I would come home, take my nap, and proceed to my afternoon routine. Some days, my cousins would eat breakfast with us and some other days, my siblings, and I would eat breakfast at their house. All my extended family ended up eating the gluten-free diet. Saturday was my laundry day; since middle school, I was doing my laundry under my mother's supervision, obviously. Just like with my siblings, my mother taught me how to do my laundry; of course, everything did not go so smooth; I threw some tantrums, I fought and argued. When I would calm down, my mother would redirect me to the same task. Some days it would take the whole day on Saturday, my mother would never give up. Sometimes, my grandma would even offer to do it for me, but my mother would refuse. I needed to learn and do it just like the rest of the kids. Once I realized that I could not escape doing my laundry, I started doing it, and I'm still doing it, and I'm grateful to my mom for teaching me this most important life skill. Sundays were our day out, visiting families after church, going out to eat, going bowling, or to the movies."

Pascal's Mom said, "When Pascal went to middle school, we found a couple of extracurricular activities to keep him engaged after school and to help him develop effective independent leisure skills. Some that he was particularly interested in including puzzles and reading. Pascal loved to read and do art. We will take one or all of these activities wherever we go somewhere to keep him busy. Pascal liked playing crosswords puzzles and word searches. Scrabble is the family's game. His older cousins tried to take him to the kitchen, but he did not like helping with cooking or baking. However, just as our other children, Pascal was part of the household chores. He was the mailman; he had to pick up the mail from the mailbox every afternoon and dispatch it throughout the farm to his uncles and aunties. He was also the trash pickup man. He had to empty all the trash cans from every family on the farm and put the bigger trash cans out every Wednesday night because Thursday was our pick-up day. We had four for the entire family on the farm. You can imagine how busy Pascal was after school. He enjoyed his household chores. I believe the fact that we all called him the mailman really boosted his self-esteem and self-confidence. This also helps Pascal with his social skills. His brother and cousins were playing basketball and football, and at one point I was very worried about what would happen if Pascal wanted to be part of any of those sports. Thank God, for me, he was not interested at all. It was a great relief for me when he told me 'Mommy, I don't think I would ever play any sport,' and I asked, Why not, your brothers and cousin are all into sports, don't you want to join them? He replied, 'No thanks mommy, it requires too much time, between practice every night or every morning and games every weekend, I cannot put myself in so much of a commitment. I would rather just go and support them in their games'."

Pascal did not like going to the gym either. His mother recalls dragging him to the gym with her from time to time whenever he gained a couple of pounds. Pascal learned to control his weight in order to avoid the gym. However, he loved swimming. His dad taught him how to swim, and they noticed his interest in the pool at a very young age. Luckily, they have a big swimming pool on the farm. He did not need any supervision while in the pool. Over the summer, they all walked to the pool, and Pascal would be the last one to return home.

“At home, I was the balance or the mediator between my two siblings whenever they argued. I would either laugh so hard or get sad, which made them get along because they don’t want me to feel that way because of their attitude,” Pascal said.

If you are raising a child with autism, you know that he or she doesn’t do well with any kind of change. What parents need to do is prepare them for changes to avoid a meltdown. Children with autism find any kind of change difficult because it disrupts their routine. Pascal, just like any child with autism, when the change happened, would either withdraw in his corner, scream, throw a tantrum, or show bad behavior, including aggression. Research states that these behaviors are common results of anxiety since children with autism cannot express their emotions and desires. Pascal stated, "that as a child, I would scream and cry or put up a fuss about any slight change. My mother loved to say that I cried every time when the family went out and cried when we had to leave from that place that I eventually adjusted to so much that I didn't want to leave."

"However, change is change for children with autism like Pascal. Even if sometimes the change consisted of just doing things a little different or adding new things in our family routine. Whenever we knew there would be a change either at school, at home (we lived with the extended family, so changes happened all the time), or with one of the team members, our family strategy to prepare, Pascal for any upcoming change was to identify and determine the specific change. If it were in school, we would get as much information as we could about the change. We were always proactive about letting him know, describing, and discussing the change so that he knew what to expect when he got to school on the day of the change. We would answer in detail any questions he had about that change. When we would have a family getaway, at a new location, we would make a picture book, or a collection of photos on his I-Pad, so that he had them available before and during the trip. On his bedroom calendar, we marked the departure date and time as well as the returning day and time, so he knew exactly what to expect during the change. On the day of the trip, we would have for

Pascal a visual timetable and a routine that explained in detail the schedule for that day. Pascal did not like flying, so whenever the family needed to fly on vacation, he would stay with one of his grandmas, either over at my mom's house, with whom he loved spending time, or his daddy's mother right there on the farm. She was his babysitter anyway. We tried everything to get him on a plane; nothing worked. So, we had to give up as long as he was fine staying behind when we were gone. No matter how predictable and prepared for upcoming changes people try to be, emergencies and accidents happen, which can lead to unexpected change as well. As we all know, life itself is very unpredictable, in case of any unexpected change, such as school being canceled because of bad weather, we would distract Pascal with something he liked, for example, his favorite snack, or more time on his I-Pad, or we will simply praise and reward him for handling the change well," Pascal's Mom explained.

All these changes are anxiety triggers for a child on the spectrum, however, it is the parents' responsibility to support and teach their child how to adjust to an unexpected change so that he or she would be able to handle it in their adulthood once they leave school or home and have to deal with the real world. As parents, we should help our children with autism understand that their routine and or structured schedule cannot always be followed. It is not an easy task when dealing with your child with autism.

Pascal explains that, "A parent once told my mom that 'it is easier said than done' with children with moderate and high functioning autism, but for children with severe autism visual schedules, timers, a visual pictures card, a calm area, and enough time to adjust and digest the change are factors that can help a child to manage unexpected change and teach him to be flexible and even receptive and tolerant to the unexpected change. In the family, my older brothers and cousins had to do some growing up fast. They took on a parenting role in order to better understand what was going on. My diagnosis gave the entire family a better understanding of autism as a condition of people with autism. They love and have empathy for people with differences. We all grew up having to deal with all levels of ups and downs. My sister played a second mom when I was younger. If I didn't listen to mom, she would come to my room and repeat what mom just said. Sometimes it was easier to have someone on her level to explain things or give her the opportunity to be in charge. Sometimes, I experienced bullying in the community before even going to school. Bullying occurred because of my differences. Fortunately, my family had always been a source of strength and inspiration for me. It was incredible how some of my siblings and cousins reacted by pushing me into their activities. They helped me with my homework. It was just amazing how they sprang into action after years of not knowing what was going on; it was a whole new world that made us all better people. We learned patience. My advice for people who have a sibling with autism is to know that they are the shadow and role model for their sibling on the spectrum. And older siblings with autism should also realize that their younger siblings typically look up to them. Children with autism should be appreciative for anything their siblings do for them because sometimes they may not imagine how much the other sibling puts in to being there for them. The lesson that the entire family learned is that, at the end of the day, when a child, or in some cases children, in the family are autistic, it's a diagnosis for the entire family, because somehow, everyone will be affected and involved, not just the child or the children with autism. According to my mom, I was very sensitive to certain sounds, textures, and tastes. I would smell any food that I was introduced to before I ate it. I would also smell any cold, cough, or allergy medication I needed to take, which was kind of weird. I wanted to wear my favorite clothes over and over, and whenever I had to wear something else, I would be upset and would not focus. The sound of a vacuum cleaner agitated me, so I would cover my ears and scream or hide in my corner. I did the same thing with the noise of the blender, the noise of the phone ringing, or the noise of an airplane. I could not stand the rain. I was always terrified when it was raining, or even when the wind was strong."

From Pascal's mom's experience, parents of children with autism should teach them patience and turn taking. They should understand that they need to have patience with people, just like they need other people to have patience with them. It is not easy, especially for those with severe autism. There is no doubt that it is very stressful and overwhelming to deal with a sibling with autism; they can be very annoying, but patience is the key. Know and understand sibling with autism. Help as much as you can. Never give up on trying to help.

"As a young man with Autism Spectrum Disorder, I found myself reflecting on both the challenges and strengths that my condition has brought me," Pascal stated.

Pascal's mother pointed out, "that parents also need to keep in mind that with the progress made on autism today, each child with autism is different, but he or she can live a happy and fulfilled life. Early therapies can help maximize their strengths and overcome some delays and difficulties. Just like with everything people go through daily, dealing with your child with autism will give you good and bad days. You will have happy days with your child's progress in reaching different developmental phases, and other days where you think there is no progress at all never give up, instead, when it happens, try to educate yourself more on the disability. Knowledge is power, they often say, and with a child with a disability, knowledge is a lifeline. There are so many organizations, agencies, and support groups available out there for parents to use."

Pascal at School

In order to learn about Pascal's life in school, he provided us this testimony. "On one hand, I struggled in my school experience from kindergarten through twelfth grade. Just like other students with autism, I had social difficulties, and, as a result, I did not have many friends growing up. Luckily for me, my siblings and cousins were always there.

On the other hand, I had a lot of academics and computer-related activities that kept me busy. I felt comfortable with math because I could easily do my assignments and homework on the computer. At the end of the day, I am very proud of who I have become today, and I cannot even imagine how being any different would have improved my quality of life or made me a better person. I cannot thank my mother and my family enough for never have given up on me. They believed, and they supported me.

“In middle school, my brothers got me into lacrosse. My cousins got me into speech and drama. Those activities enabled me to accomplish all that I have accomplished. I was able to find activities where I was accepted, and I wouldn’t have found those on my own. My siblings and cousins also became very protective and helped with the teasing and bullying at school. Siblings can be much more effective at educating their peer group than a parent.

“Growing up as someone on the spectrum, I have had a hard time making friends. I stuttered a lot and was afraid of public speaking. Every time I raised my hand to ask a question or read out loud, many of my peers would complain and attempt to force me to stay quiet. I was also made fun of because of this.

Despite the bullying and social problems, my speech skills improved, and I found friends who accepted me for who I was. Academically, I've done well in terms of grades, but my difficulties with autism have caused conflict with my school work. I disliked group work, and when classwork revolved around working with others, I tended to work alone. I had trouble with speaking in public; I was afraid of assignments that required us to present in public. This fear had turned into anxiety, and I started having anxiety attacks at night. It wasn't until recently that I was able to control my anxiety and thus to perform my schoolwork at my best. Since my last year of High School, I have changed from those days of my childhood. I have participated in multiple clubs at school, including Student Council and our National Honor Society. I have become so confident in public speaking now that I was chosen to speak as one of the student leaders. I've been able to progress so much that I have been accepted into college, but I decided not to attend college. Teachers and mentors have praised me for my accomplishments and my attitude change. I would like to thank autism. If it weren't for autism, I wouldn't be myself. I support individuality, and I believe that autism is a part of me.

"I will conclude that my time in school was very beneficial. It helped me to grow as a person. I have become much more accepting of my condition. I learned social skills, and I am less afraid of interacting with others than I have ever been. My experiences with teachers and peers have allowed me to feel very comfortable and confident in the community. I see that today, people are much more understanding, and they can tolerate who they used to consider and label as different. Thanks to the work of researchers and other specialists who made autism and other disabilities open to everyone who wants to learn or be educated. People are more aware of the special-needs population. I hope that reading my story will give people with Autism Spectrum Disorder (or their parent and families) hope and encouragement as they move through their autism journeys. I wish these individuals nothing but the absolute best.

"Children with autism lack social skills, but this does not mean that we cannot have fun. Parents should determine and find out what type of activities their child is interested in in order to make it available to him or her. There are different activities that will increase social skills while they strengthen the bond between him or her and those around them. However, with each child being unique, it is a good idea to keep the child focused on what he or she really likes. At the elementary level, find some social skill activities and games at school and at home to help build the skills that he or she needs to form relationships. In middle and or high school, look for activities that use speech and language in order to strengthen the child's ability to communicate. All these activities will help the child not fall behind, but to catch up with classmates and finally be able to plan out and follow their daily schedule and routine at home and at school. As stated earlier, early intervention is the key."

Pascal's mother advised, "As parents, we know our children better. As a parent of an autistic young man, I know from my experience that all parents of children with autism at some point feel either overwhelmed, guilty, angry, depressed, or even confused and frustrated. These are common emotions associated with taking care of a child with special needs. However, things are a little better today than they were twenty years ago. With early diagnosis and early intervention, appropriate and specialized treatment options lead to a child's progress, followed by a positive impact on his or her life outcome. Everything is now available to parents of children with autism in order to do the right thing for their children. All we have to do is knock on the right door. There is no need to be anxious. Resources and strategies are available to help the child live with his autism." From Pascal's mother's perspective, this is what his school experience looked like. "After a couple of months of therapies, the therapists evaluated Pascal's progress, and he was placed into an integrated preschool program for students with autism in a typical small special education classroom. This was an opportunity for Pascal to spend enough time in an inclusion classroom setting alongside his peers. From his Kindergarten year through his sixth-grade year, Pascal was in a general education classroom for most of the school day accompanied by a paraprofessional. Back then, it was not easy either for me or for some teachers who did not have experience teaching and dealing with challenging students. Some days I could see the teacher's frustration even if she did not express it. Today, things are different. Special Education teachers know how to handle students with disabilities and autism. As a student with autism, Pascal had difficulties with navigating some of the aspects of school, luckily his paraprofessional helped him with transitions from one class to the other and focus and listen in class as well as during connections. Without the support of his paraprofessional, Pascal would have struggled with transitioning from one activity to the next, especially when classroom routines were not followed when the teacher has a substitute. In order for Pascal to keep up with a new schedule, the teachers would let him know the day before the schedule was changed, that would allow him to be prepared in advance for any new event."

Pascal says, "In middle school and despite the support of my paraprofessional, I still experienced significant social difficulties during my time in school. During lunch or connection, students would call my peers and me names. They would even make fun of us, stating that we were slow and or retarded. Back then, I did not understand why I was being teased. Today, I understand what happened, and it saddens me because of my social skills deficit. There are things that I could not control; I understand that nobody knew much about autism back then anyway. I had friends who would stand up for me when I was in trouble, but I was still very upset. In seventh grade, I was put in a special education classroom, with special need students and special education teachers only. On my first day at the school, I sat with a group of students at lunchtime who would be my friends for the remainder of that school year. And for the first time in my life, I could hang out with a group of kids without a hidden fear that they would reject me because we understood each other. I sat with them every day. My teachers told my mother that I was adjusting well at the school and that she needed to reinforce whatever was done at school once I got home. My mother was willing to make sacrifices that were needed to keep it up. In eighth grade, I struggled to learn and follow the different rules and expectations of each teacher. My paraprofessional had to keep reminding me to get a hall pass. She always made sure I was prepared for class, and I had everything ready before the bell rang. I also struggled with basic skills like organizing my binder and following directions. To me, eighth grade was a little intense, and I found it hard to keep up with the teacher's pace. I would even say that I was overwhelmed by the daily routine of my eighth-grade day in school. However, I did meet a diverse population of students with special needs at different functioning levels. This gave me a supportive group of peers that I could rely on during my difficult times. My support group was highly important. With them, I struggled less with the transition to high school. Once in high school, my freshmen year was pretty much my adjustment year. The intense academic workload overwhelmed me, and until I was fully adjusted, my grades were below average. Luckily for me, I had the same group of students from my middle school, so we knew each other, which made things a little easy for us. However, towards the end of my sophomore year, I was getting better in my high school experiences. All of us were in the same special education classroom with special education teachers and paras. By the end of my sophomore year, I was completely adjusted, and I felt comfortable finding my way around the school. I tried hanging out with a group of new students with whom I would eventually spend the rest of high school. In my junior year, we already knew each other so well, and for a long enough time that we were able to hang out in each other's homes after school. We could go to the movies or just have sleepovers at mine or someone else's house, just like my siblings and cousins would. I had my first sleepover at the farm with my friend in high school. Can you believe it? My mom said better late than never. My siblings and cousins were having their sleepovers either at the farm with their crew or at their crew's house since elementary school. My senior year went by so quickly, and I believe I did not see the time going I was so busy having fun. The year eventually came to an end with my graduation. I felt happy and proud of myself for overcoming several obstacles, making lifelong friends, and acquiring vital academic skills. But I also felt sad because some of my friends were going out of state. We communicated through phone and text messages for a while, and then we lost contact with each other. Until this day, I think about them, and I'm wondering who they became."

The teenage years for Pascal were a time when he became more socially sensitive and aware. At that age, when most teenagers were concerned with acne, popularity, grades, and dates, Pascal became painfully aware that he was really different from his peers. He noticed that he lacked friends, and unlike the other kids around who were his age, he wasn't dating or planning for a career. His life was a combination of therapies and doctors' visits. For some students with autism, the sadness that comes with such realization urges them to learn new behaviors such as worse aggressive behavior. Pascal instead explained how the pain of feeling different motivated him to acquire more normal social skills. He wanted to sign up for club activities at school, the community, and at church. He was even part of a scout group.

Pascal Today as an Adult

"As I grew older, I could feel that I was a burden for the family. My parents were very worried about my adulthood; sometimes, they would blame each other for my condition or even get remorseful asking themselves what they did wrong or if they are being punished. As far as I'm concerned, I never stopped asking myself the question of WHY ME? Sometimes, I wish I was just a normal kid so that my family could live a normal family life. I was comforted by the fact that I wasn't a punishment, because around me tons of kids were just like or even worse than me. I was wondering why the condition is unstoppable. Research and other scientists should be able to stop autism since there is no cure to the condition. Today as an adult, I'm a better person living with autism. I graduated from high school, and I decided not to go to college. Instead, I got a job on the family's farm. I had the opportunity to work and earn an income on the family's farm where we all live. Something that I was already doing as a hobby before it became a full-time job for me.

"In high school, I volunteered in the media center, shelving books. I really enjoyed the experience since I love to read. Even now, whenever I can get a ride (since I cannot drive) to my old high school, I will go and volunteer in the same media center. As an adult with autism, I spent most of my time working on the farm, and I'm loving it. When I was younger, I watched, and I followed my dad and his brothers when they were working on the farm. Today I'm so proud to be part of the farm's staff. The other staff is a farm manager, a trainer or instructor, stall cleaners (usually over the summers they are teenagers who love horses and want to trade labor for board and riding lessons). We also hired a vet, a farrier, and a feed and hay supplier. I'm the farm entertainer. I'm also in charge of other activities such as the master of ceremony on the farm and showing the farm to tourists or students on a field trip. I will say I'm the farm supervisor.

"Here is what my typical day as a supervisor looks like: Weekdays I start off my day with a first-round checking the dispensing of hay, as well as the water buckets to make sure there is clean water available to horses throughout the day, I check to see if the stalls are cleaned, I also need to check that all my other staff are in, trainers, vet, farriers. Then I go to lunch. In the afternoon and the evening, I do my second-round supervision. I double check again to be sure that all equipment was put away and the barns are closed. I have to make sure the horses have enough water and hay for the night. Friday evenings, Saturdays, and Sundays I supervise any event that is going on at the farm. It might be either a horse show or barn parties. Sunday and Monday are typically my days off; however, I don't feel like I need to take any days off. I have so much fun working with my horses. The farm has a pony club, and of course, all the kids of the family and their friends are members of that club. We all love riding horses. I have a passion for raising horses. The club offers its members a wide range of different activities and events. They include horse and pony care competition, the musical ride competition, and my favorite is the equestrian competition. At the summer camp or during the Christmas holidays, I am very busy supervising one or all of these activities on the farm, which to the members is wonderful because they will know how their riding is coming along! People ask for horse lessons, so every summer we hold two weeks camp of riding lessons. Sometimes on Saturdays and Sundays, people rent the barn for barn parties. My job is then to verify that everything is going smoothly for them, but also that everything is being cleaned up and put away after the party. I would not trade my time with horses for anything in the world! Whenever I tour the farm, I realize how lucky I am, and I'm very thankful for that," Pascal said. "I especially take care of tourism, giving tours of the farm to visitors. I really enjoy when the visitors are a group of students with disabilities coming on a field trip or just visiting the farm with their family. I share my experience and my journey with them. That makes them feel better and gives them hope that someday, as adults with disabilities, there is a future for them as well. I have more time to spend with the horses on the farm, taking care of them, giving them directions, or just riding them for my equine therapy. By learning to care for horses, or engaging in equine therapy, people with autism learn to follow directions doing a fun activity. When a horse responds to my commands during training, that gives me positive reinforcement and a great sense of pride. During training sessions, I spent my days with horses because I'm in charge of other people with autism who take their equine therapy on the farm. Riding horses is fun for everyone who loves that activity, but it is especially fun for people with autism because it is an opportunity for them to improve and practice their cognitive and language skills, motor skills, as well as social skills. It helps even those with severe autism. Horses help calm riders with autism, allowing them to focus, think, and enjoy the training. The desire to ride and taking turns allows riders with autism to practice positive behaviors by learning to wait their turn. I have a fiancé, Marguerite Meghan. She is an autistic young lady, of course, high-functioning, beautiful, and very smart. I look forward to marrying her and starting my own family, even though I wonder if I ever have kids, will they be autistic as well? My mom is convinced that they will be just as typical as they can be. We shall wait and see. Hopefully, she is right. Once we get married, if we cannot have children of our own, we may end up adopting two or three children with autism. Anyway, time will tell. I met Marguerite through the Youth with Disabilities Program at our church. We attend the same church, so we have known each other for ten years now, and of course, both of our families have known each other for a long time as well. After Marguerite graduated high school, she attended and graduated from a sewing courses program because she loves sewing. She is a tailor. We both live on the farm, so she takes care of all the family's sewing needs; fittings, alterations, etc. She wants to open her own business. Hopefully, if God is willing, someday that dream of hers will come true.

"My advice to other people with disabilities and autism is to go to college (if they can). After high school graduation, for parents and students with autism, there are many factors to take into consideration before deciding about the future. The common question that usually comes to mind is what do I need for my child post-high school; college, a different educational opportunity, a career path, an adult day care program, or a vocational rehabilitation service. Again, there is no "one size fits all" with students with autism. Parents should know the right decision and direction for their child. Schools and state regulations and agencies for students with disabilities in general and with autism, in particular, are resources that help provide information, insights, and even assistance.

"If college is not an option, there are other educational programs and job training programs to consider. They offer opportunities based on each child's need to learn a career and independent living skills for their future as an adult. If the vocational rehabilitation is the option, there are agency and counselors who will assist in preparing for or getting employment.

"For students with severe autism, the day program might be the option. Another option that parents might consider is moving the child away from home after high school graduation. There are many choices available for people with autism when it comes to living away from home. Such as in-home services, independent living, supported living, group homes, host home, foster care homes, and respite care. Sometimes, parents opt for group homes or host homes if a child has severe behavior or the parents are getting older, and they cannot take care of their older child with autism anymore, or if they need a break. All this information about services available today for people with autism twenty-two years and older were gathered and can be found on state websites and through agencies and state service providers. This information is open to parents, families, and anyone who wants to be educated on autism," says Pascal's mother.

"My mother today advocates for autism and helps parents and families with autism learn more about how to recognize the signs of autism. There are various resources available for parents with relevant information about autism. My mother is a visual learner. She likes video resources better. Videos, she said, are practical because she could watch and learned about all the clips illustrating typical and delayed development. The videos are helpful to anyone dealing with a child or relative with autism; a parent, caregiver, relative or friend will learn the subtle differences and how to spot the early red flags for the disorder. My mother's advice to other parents is to act fast. As soon as you notice a sign, talk to your child's pediatrician. Today, all parents need is to ask questions, and they will get all the help they need. Once your child has a diagnosed, the road ahead is bumpy and long. Researchers and other autism specialist made it less overwhelming."

Conclusion

The autism journey has come a long way. Researchers and other autism specialists are working very hard to find their causes and develop appropriate and effective treatments or interventions. Early intervention remains the key for health care professionals' efforts and alternative approaches in autism are promising. Autism awareness and understanding are also very important. Public and professional awareness has improved in recent years. However, there is no doubt that awareness still goes a long way. Just as the condition itself, autism awareness should be a lifelong priority. People's awareness can have a huge impact and improve how to deal with autism from early diagnosis to treatment and support.

It's still very difficult today for families to hear for the first time that your child has autism spectrum disorder and realize that his or her life and yours may be very different than you expected. Living with autism does present challenges for the whole family. It comes like a dream, then it is a big shock, and so many questions cross your mind. How do you answer those questions in your mind? How do you get over that shock? Why us is the common unanswered question. Where to go from here? How do you know what to do next? How and when do you tell your friends and family?

Today autism programs are available, and they will help you with those questions as you and your family begin your journey through autism. Today, better than fifteen or twenty years ago, people with autism can find help. There is a combination of treatments available from early intervention, special education in a school setting, family support, and even medication, to help them have a normal life by reducing the severity and frequency of their disruptive behaviors. Medications, in some cases, are used to help alleviate symptoms such as depression or mood swings. The special education programs expand their capacity to learn, communicate, and relate to their peers while reducing their symptoms. "As a mom with a child with autism, I'm glad that research has come a long way," Pascal's mother acknowledged. There is not a cure yet. However, the life of children and adults with autism has greatly improved.

Also, today evidence shows that a child who receives effective therapies and appropriate education has every chance of recovering his or her unique capacity to learn. We've seen children who could not speak, talk after a couple of speech therapy sessions.

References

American Autism Association

https://www.myautism.org (2016)

American Psychiatric Association. (2013). Diagnostic and statistical manual of mental disorders (5th ed.). Washington, DC.

Autism Speaks

https://www.autismspeaks.org/what-autism(2016)

Howlin, P., & Moss, P. (2012). Adults with autism spectrum disorders. *Canadian Journal of Psychiatry, 57*(5), 275.

Individuals with Disabilities Education Act | IDEA https://sites.ed.gov/idea/(1998 & 2011)

Kasari, C., & Patterson, S. (2012). Interventions addressing social impairment in autism. *Current Psychiatry Reports, 14*(6), 713–725.

Landa, R. J., & Kalb, L. G. (2012). Long-term outcomes of toddlers with autism spectrum disorders exposed to short-term intervention. *Pediatrics, 130*(2), 186–190.

the reports by the American Academy of Pediatrics and the National Research Council http://www.aap.org (2018)

U.S. Center for Disease Control and Prevention (CDC 2014) (CDC 2017). Autism and Developmental Disabilities

Winner, M. G., & Crooke, P. J. (2011). Social communication strategies for adolescents with autism. *The ASHA Leader.*

Glossary of Terms

AAC Assistive Augmentative Communication device

ABA Applied Behavior Analysis

ABC Autism Behavior Checklist

ASA Autism Society of America

ASD Autism Spectrum Disorder

BSP BIP Behavior support, Behavior Intervention plan

CDC Center for Disease Control

DD Development delay

EIS Early Intervention Services

FAPE Free Appropriate Public Education

IDEA Individual with Disability Education act

IEP Individualized Education Program

IFSP Individualized Family Services Plan

MMR Measles, Mumps and Rubella vaccines

OT Occupational therapist

PECS Picture Exchange Communication system

PT Physical Therapist

SLP Speech Language Pathologist

Acknowledgments

I would like to dedicate this book first and foremost to my lovely husband, who made possible everything I ever wished. Great kids, seeing my dreams come through. You are my rock, Parfait Many. To my two sons, Rhod and Klivert Many who encouraged me to write this book. They are my world. Thank you. Also, to my late parents, Mr. and Mrs. Many, my late older brother Andre Marie, and my older brothers Nico and Emmanuel, my older sister, Christine. They all instilled in me self-confidence that with hard work, anything is achievable.

Finally, Dr. Biloa - Many would like to acknowledge the incredible team of autistic contributors for this book project: The Pascal family who wanted their names not to be mentioned to protect their privacy. To her clinical partners and other collaborators and advisers. Without whom this first book dream project would not have come through. And obviously, her personal research and professional knowledge on autism and other disabilities.